# SALES FOR PROFIT

How You Can Start Your Own
Business, Buying and Selling Items
You Choose, to Make Money
Quickly, Easily, and Affordably

# JOSEPH PESTA

# SALES FOR PROFIT
## How You Can Start Your Own Business, Buying and Selling Items You Choose, to Make Money Quickly, Easily, and Affordably

Published by Joseph Pesta

ISBN-13:
978-1519696809

ISBN-10:
1519696809

First Edition

Published in the United States of America

*To my loving family, for all of their
support, and for sticking by
me through years both thick and thin.*

# DISCLAIMER

This book is intended for informational and educational purposes only. It does not make any promises of success, nor does it seek to offer any legal, medical, or financial advice. Starting, or running, any business involves risk. It is up to each individual to decide if such risks are acceptable to them or not. The author and publisher assume no responsibility for any losses or other hardships your business may incur, nor the results of those hardships or losses. Please seek out the advice and assistance of licensed legal and financial professionals. Also, be sure to contact your state and/or local county, city, town, or other official offices to determine what licenses and/or other documents you may need to operate your business legally in your area and/or the areas you intend to do business in.

Now that we've gotten all of that out of the way, let's move on.

# CONTENTS

# INTRODUCTION

It's the dream of being independently wealthy, of being able to come and go as we please. It's the dream of not having to ask permission from anyone but ourselves when we want to take a day off from work, or go on that long vacation we've been planning for what seems like an eternity, but could never find the time to take. These are the dreams we all have when we work for someone else. How do we turn those dreams into a reality? That is a different story entirely.

Working a nine-to-five job is a great way to make a living. You'll probably earn enough to keep a roof over your head, put food on the table, and keep all of your necessary bills up-to-date. That's fine, if that's where you want to stay for the rest of your life, but the truth is most of us don't.

If you want to get ahead, make your fortune, and live the life you've always wanted, working for someone else is most likely not going to get you there. How, then, can you reach your goals? The answer is simple, really. It's up to you to take action. It's up to you to start your own business, and start working for yourself.

I know, I know. You probably think I'm crazy, right? You're probably starting to wonder what kind of shady, money-making scheme is he trying to get me involved in? If that is what you're thinking, I can assure you, you couldn't be more wrong.

Starting your own business isn't as difficult as you may think. Frankly, it's really very simple, especially in the times we live in. Never has it been more possible, more simple, for a person to bring their ideas to life, and build a business that can not only support them, but help them reach whatever goals they set out to achieve. I know of many people who have done just that for themselves, and are quite successful at it. You could be, too, if you're willing to take the chance.

Since you've opened this book, and read this far, more than likely you're ready to make the leap that will put you where you want to be. In the chapters that follow, you'll find that the simple business of making sales for profit is a business just about anyone can start up on their own. Not only is it fun, but it doesn't matter where you live, how old you are, what sex you are, or what your social or ethnic background is. All you really need is a small area of your home to get your plans rolling, and the confidence, drive, and determination to make your dreams come true.

Come with me now, as I introduce you to the business of buying and selling for profit. By the time you reach the end of this book, you should be ready to go out, make your fortune, and start living the life you've always wanted.

# CHAPTER ONE
## *What's It All About?*

Okay. You've bought this book, you've read the introduction, and now you're ready to go. So, what's all this about sales for profit, and buying and selling? What is it, and how can it help me? Let's take a look at each of these questions, and answer them in turn.

Sales for profit, or buying and selling items for a profit, is basically what each of us experiences every time we go to a department store, a grocery store, or any time we buy anything from anybody, anywhere. Simply put, it is the business of buying merchandise at reduced or wholesale prices, then selling it for a profit. How much that profit will be, depends on how high or low you decide to set your prices.

You don't have to be one of the big chain stores to buy items at reduced or wholesale prices. You don't even have to buy merchandise that already exists at all. If you have an idea of your own for a product that you can make yourself, or if you can create items to sell that come from doing one of your favorite hobbies (such as painting, baking, gardening, woodworking, etc.), then you're already halfway there.    If you can't make something yourself, don't worry.    There are hundreds, even thousands, of things you can buy at reduced prices, then sell yourself and still make a lot of money.    We'll delve into these ideas more in the chapters ahead.    Right now, let's take a closer look at how this business works.

When you go to a store, and buy an item, whether it be clothes, food, toys, electronics, or furniture, the store that is selling you the merchandise more than likely paid at least half of what you paid for it, or less.    Surprised? Don't be.    It's true, and it happens every day.    What is surprising is that most of us don't question it at all.    We just buy and buy, and the owners of these stores pull in more and more money.    Am I right?    So, why can't that be you pulling in all of that money, just like the big chains of stores you're used to shopping at?    Well, it can be. That's the point.

Stores know that you need what they have, and the smart ones make you think you're getting a better deal with them than you are with their competitors. How do they do this? It's done all sorts of ways. The way most of us are familiar with is through the big storewide sales that we see advertised online, in newspapers, and on television. But those big bargains you think you're getting aren't always what they appear to be. Let's take a look at the following example, and I'll explain.

| Shirt Costs: | Store Paid: | Price At 50% Off: |
|---|---|---|
| $40.00 | $10.00 | $20.00 |
| | | (The store makes back the $10.00 it paid for the shirt, plus $10.00 profit.) |

**Example of Profits Made
From 50% Off Sale At Store X**

Let's say you buy a shirt at Store X, and normally it would cost you $40. Now, let's say that just above the rack you picked that shirt off of, you see a sign that says 50% off. You think, "Wow! Fifty percent off. What a great deal. I'll only pay $20." The seller has you hooked. But are you truly getting the big deal you think you are? Is the seller just giving the merchandise away? Not at all. What if the seller bought that same $40 shirt from the manufacturer for the reduced or wholesale price of $10? He or she would still be making a profit from the sale, because after they bought the item at a reduced price, they marked it up four times what they paid for it, and now they are making a $10 profit. Sure, they might not be making as much as they could have, had you bought the shirt at full price, but the reduced prices bring more customers into the store, and Store X makes more money than it would have by increasing the amount of purchases made through the use of the 50% off sales tool.

So, what does this have to do with you? It shows you that no matter what kind of merchandise you will be selling, you can usually make a profit on it. Even if you choose to cut your own prices and create your own sale, or if sales are slow, and you're forced to really slash the price of your merchandise to what it cost you to make or buy it, you should be able to at least make a small profit or break even, and still have enough money to buy something else and try again.

What I'm trying to show you here is that just like Store X, by buying or creating merchandise, then selling it at a profit, you can make big money in less time than you might think, and have a lot of fun in the process.

What's this, a business that's both lucrative and enjoyable at the same time? That's right. Whether you love to shop, or you love to make things on your own, working in this business doesn't have to seem like work at all. Let's say you decide to make your own merchandise by working at a hobby you may have had for years. Only now are you realizing that your hobby can also earn you a very sizable income. Since this hobby is something that you've enjoyed already in the years previous to your starting up your own sales for profit business, then doesn't it stand to reason that you will continue to enjoy it now that it is providing you with the merchandise you will use in your sales?  Of course it does.  In fact, you may find that as you begin to make money in your new business, you will begin to enjoy that favorite hobby of yours even more.

As I stated earlier, having a hobby and making your own merchandise isn't the only way to find products to sell in the sales for profit business.  As a matter of fact, I know of several people that only buy existing merchandise that you can find in stores, directly from the manufacturer, then sell it themselves at prices below what a customer would find it for outside.  Not only that, but many of these sellers manage to acquire quite a few hard to find items that they then offer to their very pleased customers at a fair price.  The customers are happy, the seller is happy, and the seller's business makes money from the sales.

If buying existing merchandise is the route you prefer to take in this business, that's great, too.  The only difference between buying products that already exist and making products yourself, is that you'll have to do a little more hunting around to get just what you want if you buy the products from a manufacturer. Don't let that discourage you, though. Just because you may have to do a little legwork, or make a few phone calls, doesn't mean that acquiring your merchandise will be impossible. The truth is, many times searching for what you want, and then finding it, can be just as satisfying as if you made the merchandise yourself, then stood back and looked over your work, feeling proud about what you accomplished. When you find that particular piece of merchandise you've been looking for, you'll feel every bit as proud about your achievement as the baker, the gardener, the crafts maker, or the woodworker feels about theirs.

Now you've got an idea about what this business is, and what it can offer you. Let's move ahead to the next chapter, and talk about what you will need to get your own business started.

*"There is no bigger failure
than never trying."*

*- Joseph Pesta*

# CHAPTER TWO
## *Getting Started*

As I stated in the introduction and the previous chapter, the sales for profit business is an easy one to start up by yourself, or with the help of another. Whichever way you choose to go, being sole owner of your new business, or teaming with a friend, relative, or spouse, the three most important things you will need (aside from the merchandise you will be selling) are drive, determination, and commitment.

**Drive:** You *must* be willing to expend the energy it takes to make your new business soar, and you must be willing to take the risks that come with starting any new business. Whether it be this business or any other, starting a new business always involves risk. It's up to you to make sure that the risks you will be taking are sensible ones.

**Determination:** You *must* be determined to succeed in your new business, and make others believe that what you have to offer is something they need, and something you are willing to give them a fair price on.

**Commitment:**    You *must* be committed to your business at all times.   Even on those occasions when sales may become slow, you must stay committed to your new endeavor, and have confidence that things will pick up again for you, because you are determined to make it happen.

### *What Are the Risks?*

Before you get started, there are a few things you need to know.  As stated above, the starting of any new business involves a fair amount of risk.  It is those who are willing to take those risks that will reap the most rewards.

Taking risks, though, doesn't mean taking foolish risks. It merely means that whatever you decide to invest into your new business, you should also be prepared to lose.   I know that some of this may sound a little discouraging, but it wouldn't be fair if I didn't tell you these things in the beginning, before you invest your money in the merchandise you plan to sell.

The success of any new business depends largely on the person, or people, starting it. The success of your new sales for profit business will depend largely on you, and the merchandise you choose to sell. The thing to remember here, is not to start too big right away. **<u>Don't</u>** quit your job, if you have one, and invest all of your money in any product before you know if it will sell for you or not. What you want to do right in the beginning is start small, test the waters a little, then slowly begin to expand your business as sales increase.

If you take my advice, and start by doing a little at a time, you won't be sorry. If all goes well, you can always begin expanding as you see fit. If sales don't take off, however, at least you wouldn't have put all of your money into one product you can't move. Just remember, the great thing about the sales for profit business is that you make your own work schedule. It can be full-time, part-time, or just occasionally when you need the extra money. It's up to you. You control how big you want your business to become. By exercising a little caution up front, though, you'll stand a much better chance of making your dreams happen that much sooner.

### What Will I Sell?

Before you do anything, the first thing you'll want to do is decide what kind of merchandise you want to sell. Do you want to sell a single product, or do you want to sell a variety of products? Will these products have any relation to each other? For example, do you want to sell crafts you've made yourself? If so, do you want these crafts which you made to be your only product, or do you want to sell the patterns you used, and maybe even the tools you used to make them, as well? Do you want to sell toys that you've purchased from a manufacturer? Do you want to sell just a single line of toys, or do you want to sell a variety of toys? Will these toys be related in any way? For example, are they all action toys, cute stuffed toys, or toys for children of only certain ages? As you can see, the choices are limitless, and the same questions can be asked of just about any other product you can imagine.

## Choosing A Name

Your first choice is to decide what you want to sell. The next choice you'll need to make, is what do you want to call your new business. This choice may be just as important as the choice of what you want to sell, because if people are turned off by the name of your business, or simply can't seem to remember it, the results could be lost sales. And lost sales means lost money, your money.

When choosing a business name, keep in mind what it is that you are trying to sell. This can be very helpful. Try to choose a name that sounds pleasant, one that sounds professional, and try to make sure that it isn't too difficult to pronounce. After all, if people can't pronounce your new business name, chances are they'll stop trying. You don't want that to happen. You want people to remember the name you've chosen, and you want them to remember you. If a customer buys something from you once, and remembers who sold it to them, and that the experience was pleasant, chances are that customer will buy from you again.

Your business name is what potential customers usually notice first. Like first impressions, you want to make a favorable one. Try choosing a name that relates in some way to what you're selling. This way, when people remember the name, they also remember what it is you sell. If this doesn't work for you, then try to choose a name that will complement the business, yet stays close to what your main focus is. In other words, if you're selling food products, or simple crafts, the name *Z Technologies* wouldn't make much sense.

Whether the name you choose for your business is a catchy one, or one that makes your business sound important, the absolute of any business name is that it must sound professional. Whether you buy your merchandise at reduced prices from others, or create it yourself, in the sales for profit business you will undoubtedly be dealing with other business people. These people may be the people you buy your merchandise from, or the people in charge of the location where you will want to sell your products. Whatever the case, most likely they will be professionals, and they will expect you to be one, too. If your business name makes you sound unprofessional, there's a good chance other businesses won't want to work with you. You can't afford to let that happen.

When you name your business, try to make it sound like it's bigger than it is. It doesn't matter how big your business really is. You could be running it from your dining room table. The key here is to not let everyone else know that you're running it from your dining room table. I know it shouldn't matter where you run your business from, or how big the business really is, but the sad truth is that there are still some people out there that do care. Sure, it's a form of snobbery, but the fact is that is does still exist.

Home businesses are becoming more common every day, and many people won't care if you run your business out of your kitchen, your dining room, or your garage. Others will care, however, so it's better to let them think your business is bigger than it is. After all, you may have to deal with other businesses from time to time that have this attitude toward smaller businesses, so it's better to be safe than sorry.

Now, I'm not saying that you should lie when you come into contact with other business people. Never do that. I'm merely saying that what they don't know won't hurt them. Of course you won't want to pretend that you have a multinational corporation when you really have just a few items tucked away in a spare closet. That would be deceitful, and it would reflect poorly on you if the person you were speaking with found out the truth. The easiest way to get around the question of what size your business is, is to simply not offer any information in that area if not asked directly. As long as you conduct yourself and your business as though you were that big multinational corporation, then most people will be happy with the service you are providing, and not care about these trivial matters.

### The Legalities of It All

Once you've decided on the name you want for your business, the next step you should take is to check with some of the various agencies in the state that you live in, to make sure that you get all of the forms and other paperwork that you will need to fill out to make your business legal in the eyes of your state. Try asking questions of your local office of the State Board of Equalization, the SBA, the County Clerk, or even an attorney if you know one. If you ask them for advice on the steps you should take in order to make your new business legal in your state, someone should be able to help you.

Different states have different laws as far as businesses are concerned. Some states require that you collect sales tax with every sale you make to fellow residents of your state. Other states have certain zoning laws that may apply, depending on what type of business you run. Whatever the case, it's always better to be safe wherever the law is concerned. A few phone calls now could save you dozens of headaches later.

In addition to making sure you have all of the paperwork you need to operate your business legally, you'll also want to make sure that the name you came up with for your business isn't already being used by someone else. This type of situation doesn't happen often if you've done a little research up front when deciding on a name for your business, but it does happen. Check with the County Clerk's office in your state, or it's equivalent, for advice when you go to register your business name with them. You can also seek the advice of an attorney, to make sure you aren't infringing on any trademarks or other items by using the name you've chosen. Though it may seem like a lot to do, taking care of these steps now can save you a lot of time later, and you'll then be reassured that your new business, from here on in, will be completely legal.

### Where Do I Get My Merchandise?

So, you've decided what you want to sell, you've chosen a business name, and you've taken care of all of the paperwork the state you live in requires you to fill out in order to start your business. Now, it's time to start building your inventory. Your inventory for your new business can come from any number of sources. You can make products yourself, you can buy products at reduced or wholesale prices that other manufacturers already make, you can scour the classifieds online or in your local newspaper, hunt through flea markets and garage sales for items you can buy, fix up, and sell at a profit, or you can go through your own belongings and see if there is anything you don't particularly need anymore, but are reasonably sure you could get a good price on. All of these ways are great ways to build your inventory, and all of them can bring you the profits you're looking for.

If you intend to make everything you will sell yourself, then all you need to do is get to work and start creating. If you intend to search the classifieds, flea markets, garage sales, or even your own house, then all *you* need to do is start hunting. If you intend to sell products that already exist, which are made by other companies, there's a little more involved.

Let's say that you've just gone to your local shopping mall, or shopping plaza. While you were there, you saw a group of T-shirts you think would be great to include in your inventory. The only question now is, how do you get those same T-shirts the store you were in had, and how do you get them at a low enough price that you can either sell them for the same price the store was selling them at, or sell them at a price that is even lower than the store's price, making customers realize that you have the better deal? The answer is easy. You need to find out who the manufacturer of the T-shirts is. How do you do this? Read on.

Most products you see in the stores, even products you have in your home right now, have the name, as well as some type of online or physical address, of the company that manufactures the product somewhere on it. It's not always easy to see at first glance, but if you check the back, bottom front, side, or underside of the item you're interested in, you'll probably find at least the name of the manufacturer, if not more. In our T-shirt example, just inspect the front and back of the tag inside the shirt's collar. That's the most likely place the information you want will be. If you do all of this, and you still can't find the information you're looking for, try looking at other items with the same name. If you were looking at a particular toy, for example, and couldn't find the name of the manufacturer, you would then try to find other toys from the same product line, and inspect their packaging as you did the first item. If all of your inspections turn up nothing, then you could always try asking the store manager who makes the item you want. It's possible that they may give you the information you need. True, it sounds like a lot of work to go through just to get a name and address, but it's not always that hard. Once you get the information you're looking for, at least you can be proud of the fact that you did find it.

Okay. You have the information you were looking for. Now, what do you do with it? Let's go back to our T-shirt example.

With the information you have about the manufacturer of the T-shirts you wish to buy for your own inventory, the next step you'll take is to get in touch with the manufacturer of the T-shirts, asking them to send you a catalog of their products. This can be done through a phone call or through email in most cases. Just explain that you are interested in acquiring some of their products to include in the inventory of your business. Usually, if the manufacturer has a catalog of goods, or any other sales information, they'll be happy to send it along to you, or direct you to where they have it online so you can download it for yourself. If they don't directly sell their products to dealers, then they will usually refer you to a distributor that warehouses and sells their products for them. In this case, it's the distributor that would then give you the sales information you requested. After you receive the sales information you requested, it's just a matter of finding what you want in the company's catalog, seeing what the discount rates are for the amount of T-shirts you want to buy, and making an order for them.

There's usually a discount rate offered to businesses that want to make large purchases. Be sure to make it known to them that you are a business, so that you will receive their dealer prices and information, not just a regular retail catalog without discount information. Remember, you're a business now. You're entitled to the same discounts the big boys get, if your order is large enough.

If you do get sales information without discount pricing, and you're interested in buying something, don't hesitate to call the company and ask them if they offer any discounts to dealers. Most times they do, and they'll be happy to tell you about them.

Before you do any of this, though, there are still a few more things we have to discuss in the following chapters before you will be ready to start making calls and sending out inquiries. For now, just start gathering a list of the places you'll want to contact, and keep it handy for when you're ready to go. The work you do now, compiling your list of manufacturers, will save you lots of time later on.

*"True success is defined by you.*
*Know what goals you want to achieve,*
*and go after them."*

*- Joseph Pesta*

# CHAPTER THREE
## *Location, location, location...*

Now that you know what you want to sell, and have already taken the first steps towards building your inventory, your next decision to make is where to sell. In that regard, you have numerous options, including various online outlets. Before we jump straight into the online options, however, let's first take a look at a couple of the more traditional methods you may wish to consider.

As mentioned in the previous chapter, under where you can find your merchandise, a garage sale or flea market could be some of your best options, depending on what you sell.

If you've decided to go the route of gathering various items from around your own house, from the classifieds, or other flea markets and garage sales, then most likely you will end up having the sort of merchandise that would do fine in most of these venues as well. If you make your products yourself, or acquire them from an outside manufacturer, then you might want to consider leaning more towards selling at flea markets, rather than holding your own garage sale. Before you decide which route to take, know that these aren't the only options open to you. We'll discuss some other places where you can sell your merchandise a little later in this chapter. Right now, let's look at the advantages and disadvantages of these first two options.

### Garage Sales

Holding your own garage sale can be quite profitable, depending on what you sell, when you sell, how many people attend, and how low you've set your prices. Most garage sales offer a mixture of different items, so if that's what you've got, then a garage sale may be for you.

Some of the advantages of holding a garage sale are that you're right in front of your own home, and you don't have to pay for the space in which you intend to sell the merchandise you've acquired. Depending on what types of items you sell, you can make a good amount of extra money for yourself, and if you want, you can turn right around and do it all again the next week. Just be sure to check with your city or county to make sure they don't have any restrictions about how many garage sales you can hold during a month, or year, if you plan to hold them frequently. After that, all you need to do is make sure that you're able to keep supplying merchandise customers will want to buy, keep that merchandise at a fair price, and make sure that the items you sell are in good condition. If something you're selling does need to be repaired, be sure to point it out to the customer before you make the sale. Before you start planning your garage sale, though, be aware first that there are some disadvantages as well.

Customers who attend garage sales expect substantial savings on just about everything they buy. Depending on what you are selling, you'll have to be very careful that you don't end up giving away everything you have at cost or at a price that is too close to it. People who frequent these events like to bargain. Depending on what type of person you are, haggling over prices with everyone that wants to purchase something may not be for you.

Another consideration to make is the weather. If you live in a cold climate, then selling your goods outdoors in the winter is most likely not going to happen. The same can also be said for excessive heat during the summer. Even if you don't live in a cold climate, or an extremely warm one, it could always rain. Rain, after all, can come all year around, and if you get trapped outside when it starts raining, it could prove to be disastrous for your garage sale, not to mention the damage it could cause to your entire inventory.

Another factor to figure in when considering a garage sale is that there are no guarantees about how many people will attend. There aren't even any rough guesses. Have you ever driven past a house holding a garage sale, only to see the people holding it sitting outside, looking as if they've been there for days? Believe me, you don't want that to be you.

I, personally, have nothing against garage sales. Under the right circumstances they can be fun to hold at your home (or the house of a friend, if you live in an apartment or condo), and they can make you a decent amount of money.

As with any venture, though, forewarned is forearmed. If you are considering selling your merchandise at a garage sale, then there are a few things you should remember. First, plan the display of your merchandise so that it is easy for customers to get to, and easy for you to keep an eye on. You don't want anyone wandering off with any of the things you worked so hard to acquire or make yourself. Also, make sure that everything is marked with the appropriate price, and placed in a location on the item where it can be easily seen by the customer.

The second thing to remember is to try to be reasonably sure that the day, or days, you've chosen to give your sale are days where the weather conditions outside are exceptional, and not going to deter anyone from coming out to see what you have to offer. Third, always start your sale as early as possible. People who frequent garage sales often visit many sales in the same day. Don't get passed over because you started too late.

Fourth, remember to get the word out about your sale. Place signs and flyers announcing your garage sale everywhere you can think of throughout your neighborhood and others. After all, in order for people to attend your sale they first have to know that there will be a sale to attend. Fifth, and finally, always make sure to mark up your prices just a little more than what you really want for them. This way, when it comes time to bargain, you'll usually end up with the price you expected. Don't go overboard, though, but don't forget to figure in your profit. You don't want your prices to scare away potential buyers. You just want to mark them up a little bit, so there will always be room to negotiate. We'll touch on this again a little later.

### Flea Markets

Flea markets are similar to garage sales in some respects, but there are some major differences, too.

Whether you have a variety of products to sell, one product to sell, or items you bought from a manufacturer, which you intend to sell for slightly less than customers can find them in stores, the flea market outlet is usually a good way to make a lot of money in just a few days.

Besides the reasons mentioned above, of not mattering just what type of merchandise you intend to sell, flea markets offer dealers a way to showcase their products to a wide variety of shoppers in a setting that is much larger than your front lawn would normally ever be.

Large flea markets, in most areas, are usually held in an open, outdoor area, designed to accommodate thousands of people at a time, usually a football stadium or other sports arena. The event is typically held on weekends (sometimes every weekend, sometimes only twice a month), but over the typical two or three days in which the flea market is running, sales for your merchandise could be phenomenal, ranging in the hundreds or even thousands of dollars. Not bad for two or three days of work.

Dealers will typically have to pay a fee for an area in which to sell their merchandise. The day is then spent making your sales to the patrons of the event. Fees for renting space at a flea market vary, depending on just how much space you'll need, and how many days you plan to attend. If you wish to rent a large area, of course your fees will be higher. Smaller spaces, on the other hand, will run you less. Events such as these are often advertised on your local television stations, as well as online event calendars and city guides. Sometimes want ads for dealers for these flea markets can also be found in your local newspaper. To find out the going rates for space at these events, call the people holding the event, or visit their website to view their prices. Typically, you can rent space anywhere from $50 to $500, depending on how big the event is expected to be, how large of an area you will need, if you'll be renting on an ongoing basis or not, and what other accommodations you might require. When you consider the money you stand to make by selling your merchandise at one of these events, however, even a fee of $500 may be a wise investment if you can afford it.

Another advantage of the bigger flea markets is that you can almost guarantee that a large number of people will attend. Unlike a garage sale, where you can never really be sure if anyone is going to show up, these types of events can speculate in advance about their numbers, due to how many people have attended before. And believe me, those numbers are usually quite large. After all, you don't rent out an entire football stadium to hold one of these events in if you don't expect a lot of people to show up. And remember, every one of those people that docs attend is a potential customer for you.

People who attend these events are usually required to pay a small ticket fee at the door, in order to get in. Groups usually number in the thousands, and once inside they're eager to buy, and always ready for a great deal. If you're selling something just about everyone will want, your profits could be enormous.

Some of the only disadvantages about flea markets are that they are usually outdoors, inviting the risks of bad weather and low customer turnouts on those days, and you usually will have to provide everything you need to sell your merchandise yourself. Tables to place your goods on, and chairs to sit in for the day, aren't always included. Neither is Wi-Fi, so if you plan to sell at a flea market, make sure you ask what's provided when you rent your sales space. If you need something that's not included in the price of your rental fee, don't forget to bring it with you when you go.

If you do plan to sell at flea markets, some of the rules that apply here are the same as those that apply to garage sales. Again, make sure everything is easy to get to, and marked with a price tag, of some sort, that is easy to see. Make sure you have a good view of your merchandise to discourage any potential shoplifters from making you their target, and don't forget to bring along the folding tables, to display your merchandise on, and chairs to sit in, if you need them.

One last thing about flea markets, before we move on. If you plan to sell at events such as these, be aware that the big, arena sized flea markets aren't the only ones out there. In many cities and towns across the country, there are several indoor and outdoor flea markets of varying sizes that could prove to be just as good of an outlet for your merchandise as the larger flea markets. Always try to attend the biggest flea markets when you can, but during those weeks when the bigger events aren't being held, look into selling at smaller flea markets around your area, and in other areas which you can get to without too much difficulty. After all, your goal is to make as much of a profit as you can through the sales of the items you acquire. Money is money, and money from a small flea market is just as good as money from a larger one. Sometimes, the rental fees for selling space are cheaper, too, if you're having trouble getting up the fees for the larger events.

\* \* \* \* \* \* \*

Those are some of the advantages and disadvantages of garage sales and flea markets, two of the most popular ways to sell your merchandise for a profit. As stated in the beginning of this chapter, though, they are not the only ways. Here are a few other options you may want to consider, when looking for the best market to sell your products.

### *Conventions*

If you have specialized merchandise, meaning items that can be grouped into one or more categories, conventions are great places to sell from, and one of my personal favorites.

Conventions often work like the large flea markets, but usually on a grander scale. They are mostly events which cater to customers interested in specific types of products. Like flea markets, their sizes vary, and so do their fees, but if you have merchandise that can be sold through a convention, by all means, do whatever you can to attend.

If I sound like I am endorsing conventions, then you're right. I've seen the money that can be made, and its not something to be ignored. Customers that attend conventions come ready to buy. Some even save their money for months in advance, just so they can be sure they won't miss out on purchasing items they're interested in when they get there.

The people attending are usually very pleasant, since they are in a place surrounded by things that cater to their likes and interests, and when they come in, most don't expect to haggle over prices. They simply pay whatever price you're asking. All in all, the whole atmosphere is usually quite pleasant.

Now, I'm not saying that all conventions are like this, just most. As with anything, though, there are bound to be a few bad apples in the bunch. If you find that a convention you attended falls into this category, then simply make it a point not to attend it again.

Conventions are a breed all their own. Like stores, there seems to be one for just about everything you can imagine. From crafts to comic books, from all types of memorabilia to electronics, if your merchandise falls into a specific category, you're bound to find a convention that's just right for you. Sometimes, even conventions that don't seem like they're right for your product may be.

I've often seen books, toys, T-shirts, and even videos being sold at comic book conventions and science fiction conventions. The reason why, is because these items are either related to the comic book or science fiction genres in some way, or appeal to fans of both genres of entertainment. The thing to remember here is that if it's related, it can be sold at the convention.

Conventions are mostly held indoors, and patrons usually buy tickets in advance, or at the door, to get in. As a dealer, you will have to rent your selling space for the amount of days you wish to attend the convention, set up your merchandise, and wait for the customers to come to you. Fees tend to run similar to the larger flea markets for bigger conventions, and less for the smaller ones.

If you have a lot of money, and have decided to manufacture electronic items, for example, and want to sell them to the buyers of major stores across the country, then fees for these special industry conventions (aka trade shows) could run into the thousands of dollars for the smallest selling areas offered. This, of course, is just an example. Most of you will probably be selling at conventions open to the public, where booth space will start from around $100 to $350, so you won't have to worry about that.

The advantages of selling at conventions are they are almost always held indoors, so you and the customers won't have to worry about the weather, dealers are usually treated very well by the staff running the convention, tables to display your merchandise, and chairs for you to sit in, are usually provided for you, and there is often a good amount of security, so you can leave your merchandise set up overnight, and not have to worry about it being stolen. This, alone, is an added bonus, because if you have an elaborate display, being able to leave it set up, saves you the time of tearing it down and setting it back up again, day after day. All you'll have to do is show up the next morning, and you're ready to go.

If you're interested in selling at a convention, here are a few things to remember. First, price everything, and try to make the selling area you've been given as attractive as possible. Plan your display, and do a rough setup of it at home to work out the flaws. When you get to the convention, you won't have to go through so much hassle to get your selling area to look the best it can. Remember, a pleasant display is always something people won't mind looking at. If your area looks attractive, you're more likely to draw in customers, rather than if it were just thrown together haphazardly.

Secondly, be sure your setup and tearing down times, as well as the mobility, of your display and merchandise is as efficient as you can make it. Organizers of conventions often rent out facilities to hold their events in, and on the last day of the convention, they are usually hard pressed to get everyone out of the building as quickly as possible, due to additional costs and insurance concerns if they have to remain on the premises longer than they've agreed to. Being able to move out everything that belongs to you in a hurry will be beneficial to you, the organizers of the event, and it will make everyone happy.

### Consignment Sales

If you have a single product, which you made yourself, and you want to sell it in stores around the area you live in, then selling your merchandise through consignment sales is one possibility you can consider.

In this form of sales, you get a store to agree to display your merchandise in their store. When a sale is made, the store gets a percentage of the profits from the sale. What you would typically do, if this form of sales interests you, is make a list of all the stores you want your merchandise to be sold in. Don't try to target the large department stores, etc., right away. They usually get their merchandise from national distributors, and probably wouldn't be very receptive of you. Focus on smaller, privately owned stores, if you can. When you've made your list, take a sample of your product, along with any other sales information you may have that would help you, and visit the store. Ask to speak with the manager or owner of the store, then make your sales pitch to them. If the manager or owner is interested, you're in luck. Iron out your agreement with them, and get ready to deliver your merchandise. If the store is not interested, don't get discouraged. Go to the next store on your list, and try again.

Consignment sales can sometimes be used to get your foot in the door, and get your products on display in a store when trying to lease or buy your own store would simply be far too costly for you. Once in the store, if sales of your product go well, you may not have to sell on a consignment basis for very long. You may find that the store would like to make an order for more of your product, to keep in their inventory. If this happens, other stores in your area, even some of the larger ones, may become interested in what you're selling, and make their own orders from you. You'll no longer have to wait for each individual sale of your item before you see your profits. You'll be selling in bulk quantities to the stores, and you can make all of your money up front. If you can get your product into one of the big chain stores in your area, and sales go well, have the manager recommend your product to the chain's national buyers, and you could be off to a very profitable start before you know it.

### Stores and Vendor's Carts

If you have the money, you're not currently working in another job, or if you are partnering in your new business with someone who is not employed and like the idea of owning your own store, you may be interested in leasing or buying a small store (or a large one, if you can afford it), or renting a vendor's cart at a local shopping mall. This idea, of course, isn't for everyone, but even if you think it would be too expensive for you now, once you've had your business up and running for a while, and are making more money, you may just consider it.

If owning your own store appeals to you, then first you'll need to find a location for that store. Look around your area, and consider what it is that you want to sell. Try to find a site that is close by to the majority of people you are targeting as potential customers. If you make sure your store is easy to find, then your customers are sure to find you, too. Whatever your location, just make certain that the site isn't so expensive that all of your profits will be eaten back up by the costs of simply running the store.

As far as what you can sell in your new store, that's up to you. It's your store. Whether you choose to stock your store full of merchandise you created yourself, or if you choose to buy a number of different products from other manufacturers, and build your inventory from them, it doesn't matter. As long as you are selling items that people are interested in buying, and keeping them at a fair price, your customers will keep coming back.

Once you've found a location that you're happy with, simply call up the number of the leasing office, or contact the company in charge of handling the property, and get the information you need.

If a store sounds too expensive, but the idea of having your own store still appeals, then a vendor's cart may be more to your liking. Vendor's carts are the small carts you see in many shopping malls, as well as in outdoor shopping plazas. They are typically found outside of other stores, situated in the areas where mall patrons usually walk.

Vendor's carts are far less expensive than an actual store, and since you are surrounded by the mall's other stores, they offer that same feeling of having your own shop. Since a vendor's cart is smaller, however, than a regular store, you may be limited as to what you can sell. If you want to sell merchandise that is big and bulky, or if you want to sell a wide variety of items, you may find the lack of space restricting.

For someone who wants to sell just one type of product, such as dolls you created, or bird houses you built in your backyard, then the lack of space may not be a hindrance to you at all. In fact, it might even help you, by lending your business a warm, cozy atmosphere.

One of the major disadvantages about owning your own store or vendor's cart, especially if it is located in a shopping mall, is that you don't really have the freedom to take off whenever you please. Your hours are usually determined by the shopping mall's hours, meaning that you will have to be there all day, every day, if you want to keep your business running.

If this doesn't matter to you, or if you have someone that can be in the store, or at your cart, while you work at your other job during the week, and then you take over on weekends, you're lucky. If your store or cart does well, and you can afford to hire someone to be in the store or at your cart, making the sales, even better. This way, you will have the freedom to be where you want, when you want.

### *Selling Online*

Now that we've taken a look at some of the more traditional methods you can use to sell your merchandise, let's explore some of the modern ways, such as selling your merchandise online.

In recent years, it has become increasingly more easy and affordable to quickly set up a way to sell almost anything online. All you need is a decent Internet connection, a computer or some type of mobile device, such as a smartphone or tablet. We'll go over some of these devices later. For now, if you already have access to the Internet, a computer, smartphone, or tablet you're already on your way to being able to sell online.

Depending on the kind of merchandise you plan to sell, there are a number of different ways you can go about selling your items online. You can use sites such as eBay.com, Craigslist.org, or even one of Amazon.com's merchant programs to get your products in front of shoppers who are scouring the Internet looking for items just like yours to buy. With most of these sites, you simply set up a free account, take photos of the items you want to sell, upload the photos of the merchandise with a description and the price you'll be selling them for, and wait for the sales to come in. Of course, there are no guarantees your items will sell quickly, or at all. Doing some research ahead of time on the site(s) you plan to list your items on can help tremendously, by letting you see what is selling and what prices are doing the best. With eBay, for example, you can sell your items through an auction style process, where you set the starting price and the highest bidder wins, or you can choose to sell for a fixed price. The choice is yours. When you make the sale, you collect the money from the customer through an online payment service, such as PayPal, and you ship the item to the customer. Craigslist, on the other hand, is the online equivalent of traditional newspaper classifieds. Sales through their site tend to take place locally more often than not, and you'll find yourself dealing with customers face-to-face. Amazon gives you several different options to sell your merchandise, such as allowing you to ship the items yourself once orders come in, or you can send them the products you want to sell, and they will handle stocking and shipping those items for you. Each of the sites will charge fees for using their systems, but the fees are minimal when compared to the money you can make.

The one thing to remember when deciding which of these kinds of sites may suit you is to determine what kind of merchandise you plan on selling. For items where you may only have one, or only a few, sites like eBay and Craigslist are the better options. You list the item you have, and when it sells that's it. There are no more. For a site like Amazon, they're main store is more suited to the seller who has a product that can be resupplied to meet demand. If you're creating multiple units of an item to sell, or importing products, then sites like Amazon's main store site and even eBay can be good options. If you plan to have a crafts business, where you make the items you intend to sell, but may not be able to keep up with the volume a site like Amazon's main store may require if things get busy, then a site like Etsy.com or Amazon's Handmade store could be a good option for you.

Aside from selling through third party sites, you also have the option of selling your merchandise from your own Web site. Store sites with shopping carts are much more common these days, and they no longer require tens of thousands of dollars to build. Many shopping cart plugins for sites are available that allow you to set up an online store quickly, add in the products you want to sell, and begin promoting your business to get sales. Many times Web hosting companies offer some sort of shopping cart as part of the Web site plan you sign up for, and many even have plans designed specifically for sellers just like you who want to sell merchandise online. We'll discuss more about Web hosting a little later, but just know that selling from a site of your own is also an option for you.

There are advantages and disadvantages with each of the methods we've just discussed. For example, when using a third party site, such as eBay, you have the advantage of having a large number of people visiting the site and a better chance of those people finding the items you have to sell. The disadvantages are you will find yourself competing with a large number of other sellers who have the exact same merchandise as you, and are maybe selling it for less, making it harder for you to get the sale. There are also different restrictions on different sites, and you have to make sure you follow the rules so your merchandise doesn't get banned.

Having your own site has advantages and disadvantages, too. For one, you won't have the advantage of all of the built-in traffic the big third party sites have. You'll have to get that traffic on your own, through marketing and promoting your business. It can be done, but it will take time and work on your part. The advantages, however, include the site being yours. You own it. You can do whatever you want with it, and customers will only see your items when they come to your site.

As far as which option is best for you, only you will be able to answer that. It really depends on the merchandise you want to sell, and what kind of sales for profit business you're ultimately trying to create. The thing to remember with both the traditional and modern methods we've discussed as ways to sell your merchandise, is that the choice is yours and your options are limitless. What I've shown you throughout this chapter are just a few of the ways you can start selling your merchandise, ways so you can get going quickly, easily, and affordably.

* * * * * * *

This chapter has given you a look at some of the options open to you when looking to sell your merchandise to customers. If you think about it, I'm sure you can probably come up with some other ways to sell your merchandise that weren't mentioned here. Even though each idea was talked about separately, that doesn't mean that your sales for profit business has to be confined to only one method of sales.

There's no reason why you can't, or shouldn't, try to combine as many of these different ways as possible, in order to get the merchandise you spent so much time acquiring into the hands of consumers. You can go to flea markets and conventions, but while doing that, you can also try your hand in online sales, consignment sales, or even having your own store. You can do it all. If you can't afford to try more than one way of selling at first, then don't. Work slow. Build up your business, then move into the other forms of sales. There's no rush. Your first concern should be to get your business growing. How you choose to do it, is up to you.

In this business, as with any other, the bottom line is how profitable your business is to you. You want to make money, not lose it, so don't bite off more than you can chew right up front. These sales methods will always be options for you. They'll always be there when you're ready for them.

# CHAPTER FOUR
## *The Business of Business*

When starting any business, there are always a few considerations you will have to make. Things such as how you plan to run the daily activities of your new business, what kinds of equipment you'll need to get everything up and running, and how you plan to keep everything organized once you do get your new business off the ground, are all questions that need to be answered in the early stages of planning your new business, in order to save yourself some grief later on.

Fortunately for you, the sales for profit business can be kept relatively simple. Most of what you'll need is a little creativity, a little skill, and a lot of common sense. In this chapter, we'll look at a few of the things you will need to get your new business off to a great start, as well as certain items which you can purchase that can help make running your business much easier for you. We'll also discuss how you can keep your business organized, and how you may want to present yourself and your business when dealing with customers, fellow dealers, and other companies which you may have to deal with in order to acquire merchandise, sell your products, or rent booth space from at a convention or flea market.

First off, let's go over a few of the things you may want to get to assist you in keeping your business running smoothly.

### What You'll Need

When planning your new business, certain items, which for the most part can be purchased inexpensively, are always handy to have around. As you go along, you may find more of these items on your own that will get the job done easier, and much quicker, but here are a few suggestions to consider if you don't already have them.

**Computers:** Computers (PCs) are definitely more common in our homes today than they were in days past. They are also more powerful than they've ever been, they're easier to use, and they're designed with the novice, as well as the expert, in mind. The best thing is, most of us already have at least one of them, if not more.

Though some people still cringe at the thought of having to deal with any technology more complicated than their toaster, computers are an invaluable assistant in daily life, and they're indispensable to just about any business. Computers can work twenty-four hours a day, if you want them to. They never ask for a raise or benefits, they work on holidays, and they never need a vacation. Now, tell me, where else can you find that kind of help? Computers can be your bookkeeper, your tax preparer, or they can handle your invoices, your customer lists, and even give you a few hints on how to improve that business letter you've been writing, to give it maximum impact.

If you don't already have a computer you feel will be suitable to use for your business, you can usually find one that will fit your needs and budget. Beware, though. Don't be suckered into buying one that is obsolete just because the price is low. When planning to buy a computer that will aid you in your new business, the first thing to remember is that not all computers are made the same. Some are more powerful than others, some come with more features and extras, and some are so old they won't be much help to you at all. If you're in the market for a new computer, I would recommend you buy the fastest, most powerful, most up-to-date model you can afford. This is a machine you'll want to get at least several good years out of before having to upgrade again, so make sure that it isn't already close to becoming obsolete when you buy it. Price versus processing power is always a delicate balance when it comes to choosing a new computer. Make sure the computer you choose has a processor that is as close to the newest processors on the market as you can get. Try to stay away from the lower end of the scale if you can. The more recent the processor, the longer your computer should last you before it becomes obsolete.

When choosing a computer, you'll generally be faced with the tasks of deciding which style of computer is right for you, and which operating system to use. For which style, you'll want to decide if a laptop PC is going to be better for you, or a desktop PC. Each has it's own advantages. With a laptop, for example, you'll have the advantage of mobility, making it easier to use around the house, on site at a flea market or convention, or when you travel. Today's laptops are light and powerful, and can generally match most desktop PCs when it comes to the tasks you'll need to perform to run your business. Price, however, is one of their disadvantages. They are generally more expensive than desktop PCs, and their inability to be upgraded easily is another one of their faults.

Desktops PCs, on the other hand, are relatively inexpensive. They can also be more powerful than their laptop counterparts for the same price. If your budget is tight, you need something more powerful, or you don't plan on needing to have a PC with you on site anywhere or while you travel, then a desktop PC could be for you. With a desktop PC, you also have the option of choosing the size of the screen you'll be using with it. Being able to upgrade individual components as they age is also a good option to extend the life of your investment. The downside of the desktop PC is that it isn't mobile. You're confined to where you place it. If your needs change, and you find you need the convenience of mobility later on, with a desktop PC you're out of luck.

Both laptops and desktops have their place. For most business needs, and for flexibility and convenience, a good laptop will serve you well. A good desktop can also serve you well, so it really comes down to personal preference and budget when all is said and done. If you do decide to go with a desktop PC, just be sure that its components (such as processor, memory, hard drive, graphics card, etc.) are able to be upgraded easily. As the PC gets older, simply upgrading a few of these components will help you to extend its life significantly before having to buy a whole new machine.

As far as operating systems for your PC are concerned, the two most common that you will need to choose from are Windows and Mac. There are other operating systems out there, such as Linux and Google's Chrome OS, but the Windows and Mac operating systems are the most common and most widely used. For the sake of our discussion here, we'll be sticking with those two. Fortunately, both the Windows and Mac operating systems are easy to use, so once again it comes down to personal preference. There are many brands of Windows PCs, made by a number of manufacturers, whereas Mac computers are only made by Apple. The wide variety of Windows machines also offers a wide range of competitive prices, making it easier to find a PC that suits your budget. Since Macs are only made by one manufacturer, the price is the price, and there isn't much option for finding lower prices on the latest models. That being said, some people are just more comfortable using Windows, whereas some prefer the Mac operating system. In that case, the best thing to do is shop around, no matter which operating system you prefer, and find the best PC you can for the money you have. The main thing is to end up with a machine that can handle your business needs, one that you'll also be comfortable using in the process.

One accessory you'll also want to consider when buying a computer is a printer. Although most written correspondence today takes place via email, and many informational documents can simply be downloaded or sent via email in their digital form, there are still times when you may need to print documents for your own use or someone else's. For this reason, a good printer is something that is still better to have than not. Fortunately, printers are relatively inexpensive. For the purposes of your new sales for profit business, a good all-in-one color inkjet printer that not only prints, but can scan documents and photos as well, should serve you well. Try to purchase one made by a major manufacturer, as ink cartridge refills will be much easier to find.

So, you've got your computer. Now, you'll need some good software. Consult the sales people who are selling you your computer to get the software that will work best for you. Some of the main things you'll want to look at are a good word processing program, if your computer doesn't already come with one (or if the computer you already have doesn't have one built in), a good invoicing program, and good accounting software. A good tax preparation program may be of interest to you, too, when it comes time to do the taxes for your new business if you plan to do them yourself instead of using an accountant. Software programs come from many different companies. Some are better than others, and some combine features, so you only need to use their one solution instead of several different ones. When shopping for your computer, or your software, shop around, and get the best deal you can. Many big name software companies also offer online services which can be subscribed to for a monthly or annual fee, and give you all of the same features that their physical software packages offer without having to purchase a physical product and install it on your PC yourself. Many online services also have the benefit of always being up-to-date with the latest features and fixes, so you no longer have to purchase the same product over and over again just to get the latest release.

I know this is all a lot to digest about computers, but computers are like automobiles. You don't want to end up with a clunker. By following these simple guidelines, hopefully, you'll be able to find a computer that suits your needs. Now, let's take a look at a few more things you may want to have, in order to help make running your business a little easier.

**Web Site:**    Even if you don't plan to sell your merchandise online, a Web site with your own domain name is a must for any business. When dealing with other companies, or with customers, one of the first things many of them will do is look for your Web site. If you don't have one, they may not think of you as being professional, and they may choose not to deal with you on that basis alone.

Nothing says you have to have a complicated site. Just a simple, brochure-style site can serve you well. Think of it as your online brochure or business card. At its most basic, it simply needs to have a little information about the business, what it does, and how to contact someone.

The two things you will need to get your Web site going are a domain name and a Web hosting plan. Your domain name is simply the name people type in when trying to reach your site on the Web. It is typically something like nameofyourbusiness.com where nameofyourbusiness should match as closely as possible to the name you will be using for your new business. A simple Web site can then be had from most web hosting companies for a very low price per month by signing up for one of their Web hosting plans. Many hosting companies offer easy to use tools as part of your hosting plan, so that you can set up a clean, professional looking site very quickly. Another added benefit of having your own Web site, is that most hosting plans allow you to create your own email addresses. This also helps the appearance of your business, by providing you with an email address such as you@nameofyourbusiness.com which you can use when contacting other business professionals. You can then add an email signature at the end of your emails that contains your name, title, business address, business phone number, Web site domain name (URL), and any other contact information you choose to include. A small investment in this aspect of your business can go a long way, and prevent people from making assumptions about your company that can impact you negatively.

**Letterhead and Envelopes:** If you've been waiting since Chapter Two to find out why you shouldn't send out a printed letter to the manufacturer you found (in order to receive one of their dealer's catalogs, so you can order the merchandise you wanted), then you're about to find out. Before you send out any printed business correspondence by mail, you'll first want to make sure that it is as polished and professional looking as it possibly can be. How do you do this? You do this by making up letterhead and matching envelopes for your new business.

So, what is letterhead? Letterhead, basically, consists of a small business logo (usually in the upper left corner of the page, if used), your business name, address, and phone number, situated across the top of your letter. It can also be used for any invoices you mail out. The information contained here is usually done in a typeface or size different than the typeface or size of the body text, and provides the person you are writing to with all of the information they need, should they need to contact you. Not only that, but an attractive letterhead will give the impression of true professionalism, which is a must if you are dealing with other business people.

Letterhead can be created inexpensively at your local print shop or office supply store from a variety of styles. Envelopes, which have your return address printed on them to match the letterhead you've chosen, are often included as part of the deal when you are having your letterhead made up for you. Prices depend on how elaborate a letterhead you want, and how many you want printed.

Another option to having your letterhead made up outside, is doing it yourself. If you simply can't afford to have letterhead and envelopes made up, it is possible to produce high quality letterhead by using your computer, and doing the layout yourself, or by asking a friend to help you with it. With any letterhead, I recommend a good quality linen paper, in either white, off-white, or light gray. Bright colors are best not used for this purpose. Plain colors will look more professional. And don't forget, if you plan to print letterhead (or letters themselves), using an inkjet printer, make sure to find out if the paper you will be using is tough enough to hold up under the conditions inside your printer.

Remember, if you plan to correspond with other businesses, an attractive letterhead is a must. It is the first impression others will have of your business. Try to make that first impression a positive one. Once you have your letterhead and envelopes ready, you're ready to write to anyone you need to, to get the information you require.

**Business Cards:** Business cards are something no business person should be without. As you operate your business, and talk to others interested in what you do, if they ask you to give them your card, you want to make sure you have one to give. Despite the ability to easily share contact information digitally, it looks unprofessional if you've been talking about business with someone, then have no business card to give them when they ask for one. You don't want this to happen to you.

Business cards can be handed out any time you see fit to hand them out, and they can also be put on your display table when selling your merchandise, so customers can take one and have something to remember your business by. Like letterhead and envelopes, business cards can be made up inexpensively. There are even software programs for your computer, as well a online services, that can help you make them as well.

Design your business cards to match your letterhead and envelopes, whether you're going to make them yourself, or choose from one of the styles the printer of your letterhead offers. If you're unsure, let the person printing your letterhead assist you in your choice, and tell them that you want a business card that matches your letterhead. Your business card, letterhead, envelopes, and Web site should all match. Consistency is important when creating a professional image for your company.

**Smartphones and Tablets:** A smartphone is a great tool for any business. You may already have one, and you'll probably find yourself on it from time to time, contacting organizers of flea markets and conventions so you can rent selling space, contacting manufacturers to make orders for the merchandise you want to buy, and returning the calls of people who have contacted you for whatever professional reasons. Though the same calls can be made with any mobile phone, a smartphone can serve as your PC when you're away from your PC, and help you stay on top of many of your business tasks. With plans from the mobile carriers being offered for less and less, and the prices of smartphones also dropping, if you don't already have one, and can afford to get one, I highly recommend it.

Smartphones, like PCs, are made by a number of manufacturers. The two most common types of smartphones are iPhones and Android phones. iPhones are manufactured by Apple, and use an operating system called iOS. Android phones, on the other hand, are manufactured by a number of different companies, and use Google's Android operating system. Since these two types of smartphones are the most widely used, these are the ones we will be focusing on here.

iPhones and Android phones also allow their users to access online stores where apps are sold, individual programs that encompass a wide variety of interests. Users can find everything from business tools to entertainment apps, and more. For the business user, apps can be found to keep track of your mileage, your receipts, schedules, invoices, documents, and much more, all while on the go. Not only are you able to take and make calls, you can also send and receive emails directly from your device, and even take payments electronically, which we'll talk about more shortly. Regardless of what type of smartphone you get, the ability to handle so many aspects of your business from it, and the convenience that it provides you with, are indispensable.

In the space between the smartphone and the PC, falls the tablet. They, too, have changed the way many of us do business, and like smartphones the most widely used run on either iOS or Android. Like a smartphone on steroids, as tablets become more powerful many who need to work while on the go are opting to leave their laptops behind, and carry only their tablets instead. Tablets are great for handling tasks like keeping on top of email, creating documents, doing research, and keeping things like promotional materials and other business documents all in one place. They're lightweight, and many can be used while on the go, just about anywhere you can get cell phone access, depending on the model you choose. When combined with online services you may choose to use for your accounting, invoicing, and other tasks, a tablet is another tool that can be put to good use in most businesses.

If you don't already have a smartphone and tablet, are considering getting just one, or have one and are looking to add the other, it's usually best to stick with one system, be it iOS or Android, so the apps you use and the documents and other items you create can all be shared easily between devices. By doing this, you're less likely to run into compatibility issues, which will make using these devices much easier. As with PCs, when buying a smartphone or tablet, try to get the fastest, most current model possible that will do the most for what you need it to do. Make sure your tablet has the speed and connectivity you'll need for using it outdoors if you plan to use it while away from Wi-Fi. If it doesn't, then make sure if you're using it with a smartphone that it can share the smartphone's cellular connection, and that the smartphone's data plan allows for it at a reasonable price.

**Mobile Credit Card Processing Service:** If you plan to sell your products through a garage sale, flea market, convention, or any other outdoor venue, having a simple way to accept credit cards from potential customers will serve you greatly, and can even help you outdo your competition.

As mentioned in the previous section about smartphones and tablets, both devices can be used to accept credit card payments from customers. How is this done? It's done by simply using one of the credit card processing services provided by companies such as Square (squareup.com) or PayPal (paypal.com). You create a free account, and the company sends you a small credit card reader that you attach to your smartphone or tablet. When a customer wants to buy from you using their credit card, you simply swipe their card through the reader and the transaction is completed. The money for the sale is recorded, and the funds can be transferred directly into your bank account after that. A small percentage of each transaction goes to the service provider, but for the convenience of being able to accept credit cards wherever you might be selling your merchandise, the small fee is well worth it.

**Shipping Labels:** If you plan to ship your products by mail, shipping labels with your business name, address, and logo will be a necessity. Though small envelopes can be run through most printers, allowing you to do the printing directly on the envelope yourself if you choose, larger envelopes and other packaging may not fit in your printer, in which case a shipping label would be good to have on hand. They will make your packages look professional, and save you a lot of time if you have many orders to fill.

Shipping labels can be purchased and run off on your own printer if you choose. They can also be made up by your local print shop or office store. Whichever route you choose to go, just be sure the ink on the finished label will hold up during the mailing process.

**Money Box and Receipt Book:** When selling at flea markets, conventions, or even a garage sale at home, a money box will help you keep the cash you get from customers from getting lost. It will also help you with totaling up the cash sales for the day, since all of the cash will be in one place. A good money box should be large enough to hold enough bills and change so that making change for customers when selling at flea markets, conventions, garage sales, or other outlets won't be difficult. If you want to give your customers a receipt, you can always buy a small booklet of preprinted receipts, that you could then fill out when making your sales. Money boxes and receipt books can be found in most office supply stores, and they aren't usually very expensive.

**Folding Table and Folding Chairs:** If you plan to sell your merchandise at flea markets, or even your own garage sale, you'll want to have at least one large folding table, to display your merchandise on, and a folding chair or two, so you'll have somewhere to sit. After all, your merchandise will look much better if it's not laying all over the ground, and you won't want to be on your feet for hours on end, so a chair to sit in will be a welcome friend.

Folding chairs usually don't weigh very much, but be careful when getting yourself a folding table. You don't want one that is so heavy you can't move it easily by yourself. You also don't want one that's not sturdy enough to support your merchandise, or so lightweight it can easily be knocked over. Try lifting different tables and chairs, to feel their weight. Check the weight capacities as well, until you find the ones that are right for you.

**Hand Trucks and Luggage Carriers:** Hand trucks and luggage carriers are a must have when selling at a convention, a flea market, or any time you need to move your merchandise, and you simply have too much to carry in your arms. Hand trucks can be found in sizes that are easy to store, yet still capable of doing the job they need to. Luggage carriers are also great if you only have small boxes, or items that don't weigh very much. They're lightweight, they usually fold up, and storing them is very easy.

A good hardware store should have an assortment of hand trucks to choose from, and most department stores (and even some office supply stores), carry sturdy luggage carriers.

**Cooler:** If you sell at flea markets and conventions, sometimes finding the time to get something to eat can prove to be a problem. If you plan to attend these events by yourself, then the problem is even more difficult.

To solve this problem, get yourself a small cooler, and stock it with a few sandwiches and something to drink. You'll want to stay as close to your table, and your merchandise, as much as possible, and you won't always find somebody nice enough to watch over your table so you can slip away. By providing yourself with a small supply of food and drinks, at least you won't pass out from hunger. You'll be able to watch over your own selling space, and know that your merchandise is safe.

*  *  *  *  *  *  *

Well, those are just a few of the things you may find helpful in running your sales for profit business. I'm sure you'll come up with a lot more ideas to help yourself out as your business goes on.

If you find that an item mentioned is just completely beyond your reach financially at this point, don't get discouraged. These are just suggestions for things you should try to get. If you can't afford them now, you'll probably be able to afford them later, and you can get them then. Until you can afford the items I mentioned, improvise. I'm sure you'll be able to get along fine without them.

If you plan to write letters to other companies, though, to acquire merchandise through them, then try to save up your money and get some letterhead, envelopes, and business cards made. These will be most important to you, and they really do help to give your business a professional look, which is something you want to have. The main thing is to do the best you can with what you've got. The rest will come, and you can be just as successful as those who can afford to get all of the extras right away.

### *Organization*

Once you have your business up and running, you'll want to keep that business organized as best as you can. When dealing in any type of sales, good records are a must, to avoid trouble down the road with your local state agencies, as well as with the Internal Revenue Service.

Fortunately, the sales for profit business is one that is fairly easy to keep organized. Most of what is required, is to simply keep an accurate record of the money you spend for your business, as well as a record of all of the money you make through your sales. And when I say all, I do mean all.

Just because you will be selling your merchandise without someone looking over your shoulder, doesn't mean you can "forget" to include one or two sales you made here and there. Most likely, you'll always get caught, and the penalties you'll have to pay for committing these acts isn't worth the small amount (or even the large amount) of money you'll save. Remember, the IRS knows all, and sees all. The IRS is everywhere.

To keep track of all of your sales and expenses, the easiest way is to use some type of accounting software, such as QuickBooks (quickbooks.com), or one of the online services that are similar. These will allow you to easily determine how much money you're putting out, and how much your business is taking in. It also makes it easy for you, or someone else, to look over your records and compare them with how well, or how bad, you say your business is doing.

Along with accounting software, to keep track of your merchandise, your expenses, and your profits and losses, you'll also want to be sure to keep all of the receipts or invoices gathered from your purchases and sales. You'll want these for your own records, and they can help to further substantiate your claims of profits or losses should you ever be audited. Just make sure you keep all of your receipts and records in a safe place, and be sure to separate the receipts you have from your own purchases of business materials from the receipts you've accumulated through the sales of your merchandise.

When tax time comes around, if you're not sure about all of the deductions you can take, which are related to your business, try to consult with a professional tax preparer, and see if they can help you with your return so that you can get back all of the money you are entitled to.

As you can see, keeping good records is a must in this business, but keeping your inventory organized is also essential.

Regardless of how big or small your inventory is, there are a few practices you will want to follow where your merchandise is concerned. First, always keep your merchandise in a safe place. Try to keep it out of high traffic areas in your home, or cold, damp places, where your products could be damaged. A garage or spare closet in your home is a good place to keep your merchandise, but if you've ever had problems with water leakage, flooding, or insects, avoid these places, too. Look for an area of your home, or even a rented storage facility, that doesn't have these problems, and keep your merchandise safe.

Another concern about your merchandise should be how you store it. Whether already packed, or if you plan on packing it to store, be sure that the boxes or containers you use are sturdy and capable of supporting a lot of weight, if you plan to stack boxes on top of each other. After all, you don't want to crush your products, making them worthless before you even get the chance to sell them. Use padded, packing materials for fragile items, and if putting items in large boxes, be sure to use boxes that are reinforced to lessen the risk of their collapsing under too much weight.

If you plan on buying your merchandise from manufacturers, be sure to compile a list of the places you're getting your products from, and the person or people you should speak to when you contact the company. This list will become your list of suppliers, and it will always be ready for you whenever you need the information it contains. Be sure to list what type of merchandise you bought from each place, and keep it somewhere safe. If your list will be digital, instead of a hard copy, make sure you have backups. Store them somewhere safe as well. As you find new places to buy other merchandise from, add them to your list of suppliers, and update any backup copies you might have.

The most important lesson you can learn about keeping your business organized, is that no matter what kind of records you decide to keep, as long as they are thorough, your tax preparer will be happy, the state and government agencies will be happy, and your life will be made just a little easier.

### *Projecting An Image*

Your business will either falter or thrive largely on how you conduct it and by what you sell. Also contributing to its success or failure is the image your business projects.

A business that conducts itself professionally in every way stands a much better chance of succeeding than one that is disorganized and doesn't seem to know what it's doing. Your goal is to project that image of professionalism at all times, whether it be to your customers, fellow dealers, or other companies you wish to do business with. Projecting that image is simple, if you have confidence in yourself and in what you do. To explain further, here are a few of the pitfalls you'll want to look out for.

If you have letterhead, envelopes, and business cards, always make sure that their design and styles of type match. These items are essential if you write business letters of any type to anybody. They are your calling card, your first impression, and if none of them match each other, it will reflect poorly on you. Business cards and letterhead that don't match scream you're unprofessional, and professional people won't want to have anything to do with someone who's not.

Another thing to remember, is to always treat your customers with courtesy. If you're having a bad day, put it behind you while you're on the job. Customers look favorably on a business that treats them well. If treated well, they'll be more likely to buy from you again and again. Treat a customer poorly, though, and you're through. More than likely you'll never get a sale from that person again. If someone they know is considering buying from you, they won't hesitate to tell that person how badly you treated them, and you'll probably lose that sale, too. Word of mouth is a powerful sales tool. It can either work for you, or against you, with equal results.

If you plan on selling your merchandise and having to ship it to customers, then always fill your orders as promptly as possible. Customers will appreciate getting their order from you only days after they sent it in. The fewer days, the better. It shows that your business is one that cares about the people who order from it, and that yours is not just some small-time operation, but a legitimate company. If this is the image you project for yourself, customers won't hesitate to buy from you again.

Of course, always make sure the funds you receive have cleared in your account before you ship out large orders. It doesn't happen very often, but issues with bad funds are something you should always be aware of. In this business, you'll most likely be dealing with cash or credit cards, rather than checks, which should help to cut down on any problems where payments are concerned. In fact, I would recommend only dealing with those two, if you can.

Business calls must also be returned promptly if you want to project a professional image. You don't have to be tied to the phone all day. In fact, sometimes that may simply prove to be impossible. However, if you do receive any kind of business calls, be sure to contact the person right away. The person calling will appreciate that you returned their call promptly, and they'll look upon you and your business as a person and place they can trust.

Dressing appropriately is also something you'll want to make an effort to do. Just like going out for the evening, dress appropriately for the setting you'll be in. This doesn't mean that you must always be dressed in uncomfortable business attire. It simply means that you want to look your best at all times when you are conducting your business.

Whether selling your merchandise at a flea market, convention, garage sale, or visiting stores to place items on consignment, always look your best. If the setting requires more casual attire, then wear comfortable clothes, but don't dress down so much that prospective customers will be turned off by your appearance. Customers should always feel comfortable enough to approach you, not frightened that if they do they might catch something from you.

If the setting you're in requires business attire, wear it. If the setting is suited more towards casual clothes, then wear them, instead. Whichever you decide to wear, just be sure that your appearance is always neat, well put together, and never sloppy. A good appearance will reflect favorably on you and your business. Potential buyers will be more open to buying from you, simply because that added professionalism on your part makes your products look like they would be more reliable, and a better buy for the money, than products from a business that has no professionalism about it at all.

\* \* \* \* \* \* \*

The tools you need to run your business effectively, organizing your business once it's running, and projecting a business image that makes others look favorably upon you, are all vital components of your success. By keeping the simple tips offered in this chapter in the back of your mind at all times, you should have no problem convincing others of what you already know. Your business is one that is both professional and cares about its customers, and buying merchandise from you is a guarantee that any money put out will be money well spent.

*"The world is full of customers waiting to be found. It's up to you to take the steps to let them know you're there."*

*- Joseph Pesta*

# CHAPTER FIVE
*Money: Where Can I Find It?*

You want to start your new business, but you don't have any idea where you can get up enough of the money needed to cover the costs. It's a problem many of us have had at one time or another, but if you're determined enough to start your own sales for profit business, then you are also determined enough to find the money you'll need.

Money for the startup costs of your business can be found in several places. The number one place to look first is right in your own wallet. What's that, you say? It's empty? Don't worry. Chances are it won't be for long. If you have a steady job, then you have a steady income, and a few cuts here and there in your monthly budget just may give you the needed funds you've been looking for. If you don't have a monthly budget, then don't wait any longer. Make one up. Try to save a small amount from each of your paychecks. Sink that money into your business once the amount you've built up is sufficient.

Of course, you may have to cut back on a few things to accomplish this goal. First, if you eat out a lot, try cutting back on that expense by eating more meals at home. If you shop a lot, and you can get by without some of the things you would normally spend your money on, then cut back here as well. Keep going through all of your monthly expenses, cutting out what isn't necessary, then hold this money aside to sink into your new business. When doing this, though, don't cut out all of the money you normally spend on entertainment. After all, we've all got to relax once in a while, and eating out, shopping, or even going to the movies shouldn't be removed completely from your budget.

If you've made your budget, and couldn't find anything you could cut out that you didn't need, then another option that may be open to you is working overtime at your job. If you can manage to get your boss to agree to let you work a few extra hours from time to time, then this added money could be set aside solely for the use of your business. Since overtime pay is usually more than what you would normally get per hour, the extra funds could build more rapidly than simply making a few cuts here and there in your budget. If you can make a few cuts in your budget, *and* get some overtime work in, even better. You'll build your money even quicker, and be ready to start your new business sooner than you think.

People without a means of steady income can still try the budgeting option, using what money they do have, and whether working steadily or not, you can try asking people you know for a small loan to help get you started. Credit cards (as long as they are the kind that let you pay a small monthly fee, and not the kind that have to be paid off all at once every month), could be another option for the funds you need. When using credit cards to get your business going, just be careful that you don't run up too much of a debt. Start small. You do, after all, want to make sure you can still pay your bills. Buy only a few items that aren't too expensive, but can be sold for a nice profit. In that way, when you sell the items, you'll be able to quickly pay back what you borrowed from your credit cards. You'll then be able to use the profits you earned from those sales to buy more items to sell again for a profit without having to go into debt for them. You can then repeat that cycle, slowly building your business to a point where you'll be able to buy more items, make more sales, and earn more profits.

If credit cards, budgets, and overtime don't work, your family and friends will most likely be your best bet. They will often help you if they can, especially if they see your excitement about the prospect of owning your own business. If you do borrow from your family or friends, just make sure you pay them back as soon as possible. Let them know that you haven't forgotten about them, if paying them back is taking a little longer than you thought it would. This way, at least they'll be reassured that you do intend to pay them back, and that you did use the money for what you said you needed it for.

As a last resort for finding the money you need to get your business going, you could always turn to the banks for a loan. Unlike loans from family and friends, though, you'll almost always have to pay an interest fee, and if you miss any of your payments, the banks won't be as understanding as your friends or your uncle Fred. Banks often require some form of collateral as insurance against what you borrow, so that if you fail to pay, they can take something you own to recoup their losses.

Try not to jeopardize anything you own, when going this route. Exhaust every other option open to you before you risk your own security for the money you'll need to start your own business. Loans are great if you can get them, and pay them off, but if you aren't sure that you can make the payments required, try to stay away from this option, unless it's your last.

Online crowdfunding sites, like Indiegogo and Kickstarter, are also an option you can try. You create a campaign with a desired amount of money you're hoping to raise, and then you provide the details about why you're trying to raise that money, and how you plan to use it. Individuals who find your campaign and wish to contribute put a certain amount of money into it, and you wait to see if the goal you set is reached. If you choose to try this route, make it clear to the people you are telling your story to why you are seeking funding. Show them your excitement and passion. Get them involved and routing for you to succeed.

Getting money to start your business may not be easy for you to do at first, but don't give up. Try combining the different ways we just discussed to get up the money, if you have to, and see how much you can accumulate. Don't forget, you can always look for items around your house that you already own but no longer need. This can be a great way to get started, and you won't have to worry about purchasing anything. Try selling your items on a site like eBay, as we discussed earlier. Once you sell your items, and make a profit from them, you can then use that money to purchase other items to sell, or keep selling excess items you already own until you run out. Either way, keep building up those profits, and you won't have to worry about where to get funds. Even if you only have a few items to sell this way, it can bring you a lot of money quickly. In the sales for profit business, it isn't how much you have to sell, it's *what* do you have to sell, how fast can you sell it, and how much of a profit can you make on what you sell, that will keep you in business.

*"Make sure your marketing provides a clear message. Potential customers shouldn't be left wondering what you're selling, or what to do next."*

\- *Joseph Pesta*

# CHAPTER SIX
## *Promotion*

Promotion of your sales for profit business is important whether you plan to do your selling online, or if you intend to open a retail location of any kind. If you want people to know that your business exists, and you want them to know that you have, or can get, the items they want, then promotion will be a major factor in your success.

Promotion comes in many forms. It can be as simple as placing a flyer that you've prepared on automobile windshields in a parking lot, or it can be as sophisticated as running ads online, in magazines, newspapers, or even on television. How you promote your business will depend largely on what kind of sales for profit business you run, and on what kind of money you have to shell out to do it. Once again, though, you don't need to have lots of money to do this. You can easily get started with little or no money at all. The following are simply suggestions you can use to help you along.

### Sales Flyers

One of the least expensive ways you can promote your new business is through the sales flyer. These flyers can be made up by you at home, then run off at the local copy shop for little cost. Depending on how simple or elaborate you make your sales flyer, you can usually run off several hundred or more fairly inexpensively. Be aware, however, that flyers work better if you have a retail location of some type. They aren't as effective for online only businesses, or businesses that plan to do their selling at venues such as flea markets or conventions. You also need to be aware that many flyers will simply be thrown away without being looked at, so don't expect a huge return on your efforts.

When using sales flyers, leave them everywhere you can think of. Since you want to have people see your flyer, make sure it's left in places that a lot of people pass through, and be sure it's located somewhere it will be noticed. Sales flyers can still be a good tool for generating business. If you offer a few discounts on what you're selling in your flyer, it may help to generate even more business.

### Newspaper and Magazine Ads

Newspapers and magazines are another tool you can use when looking for ways to promote your business. Classified ads are often inexpensive, if placed in local newspapers and magazines. When you get more money, you can always move up to display ads for your products, and even send your ads to national publications. Even simple classified ads can generate sales for your business, and make you a lot of money for little cost.

When potential customers respond to your ads, it's safe to say they're probably interested in what you're selling. If so, more than likely you'll make the sale. To find out the rates for ads in the newspaper or magazine you wish to sell in, simply call them up, and ask them to send you their rate sheet (or rate card), or let them quote it to you over the phone.

### *Television Advertising*

If you plan to open your own store, and run your sales for profit business from there, then advertising your business on television could be the sales tool for you. Television commercials are considered one of the more expensive ways to advertise, but if you can afford it, and you want your new store to get the notice it deserves, a good television commercial is a proven sales tool in getting people interested in what you have to offer.

People tend to respond more to what they see on television than to what they read in print. It is this fact that makes television advertising as lucrative as it is. If you want your store heard about by just about everyone in your area, then making a commercial, and running it on the local stations in your area, could generate enormous sales for you.

If you're interested in running your own television commercial, call your local stations, and find out how much they charge to run a commercial in different time slots of their programming schedule.

### Online Promotion

If you plan to sell your merchandise online, then promoting that merchandise effectively is a skill you will need to learn. Luckily for you, there are many resources available to you that will make doing just that very simple.

You may already be familiar with social media sites like Twitter, Facebook, and Instagram. In fact, you may already have personal accounts of your own with one or more of these sites that you use regularly. If that's the case, then you're already familiar with how they work, and how to get your messages, photos, and other content out to people. In the same way, your business will need to do this as well. Open social media accounts for your business on the sites you like to use, and keep people informed about what you're doing. Show off your products, give them a behind the scenes look at the flea market you're attending, show them pictures of your store. You get the idea. Just be sure to keep your content more about the showing and telling rather than the selling. If your followers like what they see, they'll make the effort to visit your Web site, retail store, or find you at the venue you'll be selling at. There's no need to beat them over the head with constant sales messages.

Another way to promote your merchandise with social media is to buy targeted ads that appear on the screens of those most likely to be interested in what you have to sell. Facebook ads, for example, are a good way to do this, and will allow your ad to be seen by the masses. Make sure if you go this route, or even when simply posting messages and photos to your social media accounts, that you direct people back to your Web site, where they can easily find more information or make a purchase from you.

You can also run ads on Craigslist, and on sites that cater to your target audience. Try to be where your customers are. If you plan to sell antique items, collectibles, or some other specialty merchandise, find the popular sites that your potential customers are likely to visit. Get in touch with these sites, find out what their advertising rates are, and place an ad with them if you can.

By now you might be wondering where you will get these online ads from if you don't already know how to create them yourself. Remember when I said there are a number of resources available to you to make promoting your merchandise online very easy? Here are a couple of those resources now.

If you need ads created that will promote your business and your merchandise, you can pay someone to create them for you inexpensively. One of the least expensive options along this route is Fiverr (fiverr.com). With Fiverr, you simply search for what you need done, and you are matched with a number of people who will do what you require for only $5. Another option, and most likely a bit more expensive one, is Elance (elance.com). With Elance, you post what you need done, and freelance workers looking for projects like what you are proposing will apply for the assignment. With either of these sites, you can find many talented people who will gladly create your ads, flyers, or any other content you may need for your Web site, etc., for a relatively low cost.  They can be a great way to get quality work done inexpensively.

* * * * * * *

Advertising your business can be accomplished many ways.  Even simple word of mouth will do.  Promoting your business is key to getting as many customers as possible.  If you're starting slow, or you don't have a lot of money, don't worry.  Use social media to get the word out.  It's free, and a good social media campaign can be very effective.  In fact, there are many people who only use social media for their promotions, and they do quite well.  Be creative.  Stand out from the crowd if you can. The main thing is to do something.  Get noticed.

# CHAPTER SEVEN
## *Putting It All Together*

Okay. You have all the things you need to start your business. Your letterhead, envelopes, and business cards are prepared, and you're ready. This is it. This is what you've been waiting for. It's time to put it all together, and get your sales for profit business going.

I'll assume you've already chosen a name for your business, and gone out and registered it with the proper agencies, right? If not, refer back to Chapter Two, and do that first. What about your Web site? Do you have one? Is it updated? How is it looking? Looks good? Good.

Now that you've done that, you'll want to make sure that you have all of the merchandise you intend to sell ready to go. If you plan to make your own merchandise, then start making it and putting it together for your first sales. If you plan to buy items manufactured by someone else, then get the supplier list we talked about in Chapter Four, and either call up the people on that list, write them a short letter using your new letterhead and envelopes, or email them to request a dealers catalog with discount information.  If you want, you can include one of your business cards with your letter, so the person receiving it will be able to keep your name and contact information on hand.   If you're going to email them instead, make sure all of your contact information is in the email you send.

Occasionally, when you contact other companies for their sales information by phone, they will request that you read them the number from your seller's permit. This number is usually located near the top of the paper you received when you filed your business name with your state, county, or other agency.  The form should also say Seller's Permit (or something similar) somewhere on the paper, so look for this first if you're not sure if you have the right form.

Once you have this number, keep it ready, and make your calls.  If you plan to write a letter, instead, make sure that you know where the number is, so that you can give it later, should the other company contact you and request it.

In a few days, or a couple of weeks, after you send out your first inquiries, you should start receiving the information you requested from the businesses on your list. Once you have it, simply look through the catalogs, sites, or other information you received, and start making your orders for the merchandise you want. When you receive your merchandise, store it, and start getting it ready to sell.

If your merchandise will be acquired by hunting through local flea markets, thrift shops, garage sales, or even your own closets, now is the time to start your search. Once you've gathered everything you want, make sure everything is in good condition, and prepare your merchandise for selling.

The next step to take is deciding on your prices. You know how much you paid for each item you plan to sell. Try to set your selling price to no less than double that. In other words, if your item cost you $5.00 to buy, try to get at least $10.00 for it when you sell it, so that you will at least make back the five dollars you put out, plus five dollars profit on the item. If you plan to sell at a flea market, or are holding your own garage sale, remember to set your prices a little higher than what you want, so that when it comes time to bargain with a customer your price will be brought down to no less than where you need it to be. Remember, at the very least you need to break even. We don't want any losses here. This is a sales for profit business after all. You need to make at least some profit. To some of you, cushioning your prices like this may seem dishonest. I assure you, most people you bargain with do this all the time. The only difference is, this time you're aware of it. No one ever takes a loss when selling if they can help it. No one.

Okay. You have your merchandise. Your prices are set. The only thing you need now is a place to sell what you've made, bought, or gathered together. It's time to make the decision of where you intend to sell. Will it be a flea market? Will it be a convention being held in your area, or an area you can get to easily? Will it be a garage sale, or will it be online? The choice is yours. You can do one, or all, if you choose.

If selling at a flea market or convention, find out the phone number of the organization or company holding the event, and give them a call. Find out what their rates for selling space (or booth space, or table space) are, rent your table or area, show up with your merchandise, and start selling. When you call, remember to be sure to find out when they start letting the dealers in to set up. Be there as early as they will allow. Many times the people running the event will let the dealers in a few hours before they let the public in, to give them ample time to set up their displays. It helps in working out any potential bugs in the planning of your display, and the extra time gives you an hour or so to relax before the flood of customers comes through. If your sales go well, and you hope they do, you won't get much time to rest during the day, so take advantage of this extra time now. Enjoy it.

If holding your own garage sale is the path you've chosen, then remember to start placing your signs and flyers around as soon as possible, to start letting people know on what day your sale is being held. Set up early, get everything prepared, and wait for the selling to begin.

For online sales, you'll want to start running your ads on sites, sending out your social media posts, creating short videos about your handmade products, and whatever else you can think of, as soon as your merchandise is ready to go. Allow some time to pass before you see your first sales. If customers want what you have, they'll respond. Don't get discouraged if they have to wait until their next payday rolls around before they order from you. When those orders come in, you'll have more than enough to keep you busy, so take this time to prepare. Get your records in order, to record the sales you make, and have your merchandise ready to ship when those orders come rolling in.

If you bought or rented a store location, send out your advertising, too. Run your television commercials, announcing the grand opening of your store, or run your print ads in the newspaper or magazines, instead.

If you have a vendor's cart, run your ads. Let people know where your cart is located in the shopping mall. Get your friends and family to spread the word about your new business, too. Remember, word of mouth advertising is some of the best around, and it's free.

Make sure you're ready to go when your first business day begins, and get yourself as many customers as you can. If customers are treated well on their first visit to your store or cart, they'll usually come back to buy again, and your profits should continue to grow and grow.

Now that you are actually in the sales for profit business, and you're selling your merchandise, don't forget about our discussion on keeping your business organized. Refer back to Chapter Four if you need to, and keep all of your financial and inventory records straight. When tax time comes around, you'll be happy that you did, and you'll be ready to get even more merchandise together for your future sales.

*"The first step to growing your business is determining where you want to take it."*

*- Joseph Pesta*

# CHAPTER EIGHT
## *One Step Beyond*

So, you've been in the sales for profit business for a while now, and your profits are soaring. You're looking for a way to earn even more money, but other than continuing what you've been doing, you don't really have any ideas. Well, if you're interested, I have one for you. You know those flea markets and conventions you've been attending? Have you ever thought about organizing one of them for yourself? You haven't? Read on.

As I mentioned earlier in this book, flea markets and conventions come in all sizes. Some are held in big football stadiums, or large convention centers. Others are held in local community centers, school parking lots, banquet rooms at hotels, or even your local church. Wherever these alternatives to the larger flea markets and conventions are held, smaller size doesn't mean that a lot of money can't be made.

If you have been doing well in your new business (and I hope you have), and you're looking for a new way to earn even more income for yourself, holding your own flea market or convention could be for you. All you'll need is a location to rent out, the size of which will be determined by how much money you have to spend. After that, you'll need a little advertising, a little word of mouth, and maybe a few permits to keep the city you live in happy. The owner or manager of the location you rent out should be able to tell you what permits you need, if any. If they can't, look up the appropriate agency, and give them a call.

Once you've rented a location, you'll need to know how many tables you will be able to set up, and you will need to determine the fee you intend to charge for rentals of your selling space. To do this, gather together all of your costs for the event, then settle on a rental fee high enough to get back the money you put out, plus a little profit on the side. Add this to the price of however much you intend to sell tickets to the public for, and you should be able to make back your money, while still keeping prices fair for everyone selling at your event, as well as everyone attending it.

Now that you have your location and prices worked out, you'll want to make sure you have other dealers attending, and a variety of different merchandise being sold. Go around to some stores in your area, and in other areas nearby. Find out if they would be interested in attending. If you're holding a convention with a special theme, such as comic books, then go around to stores that sell comics, trading cards, and whatever other merchandise you think will be of interest to your patrons' particular interests. You may be surprised by how many interested dealers you find.

Advertise in the local newspapers, too, not just in your area, but in areas close by. Run a simple Dealers Wanted ad, and include a place they can call for information about selling at your convention. If you sell out all of your booth space, good for you. Just be sure to save one booth for yourself, if you have merchandise that can be sold at the event you're holding. After all, since you're running the show, and you'll be there all day anyway, you might as well make a little more money on the side.

The next thing to do, is to get the public interested in your convention or flea market. Once again, advertising can accomplish this goal. Place ads in the paper again, as well local city guides, and leave flyers around for people to take. If the event you're holding is big enough, and you have the money, you may even want to run a few commercials on television, to get the word out. If you're holding a convention for a group with special interests, and you've managed to snag yourself a special guest speaker patrons will be interested in, make sure all of your advertising states it prominently. The person you've gotten to appear could prove to be a big draw.

Try to have some type of food and drink for sale, too. If patrons get hungry or thirsty, and can find something to eat and drink while at your event, they'll be less tempted to leave, and more likely to enjoy themselves while they are there.

When you've done all you can, and you've flooded the newspapers, as well as every other form of advertising you can afford and think of, with your promotion material it's time to sit back, and hope that people turn out to attend. If they do, and you and the dealers you've rented to make a lot of money, your event was a hit. Keep the names of the dealers who rented, for future contact, should you decide to hold a similar event again. Get to know the dealers at your event, and make them feel welcome at all times. If these dealers look favorably on you now, and they see that the flea market or convention you held made them a nice amount of money, they'll be anxious to be dealers at your next event. You may even find a whole new career for yourself as a sponsor and organizer of these types of events.

*"With a good product and a message that's easily understood, happy customers and profits will follow."*

- *Joseph Pesta*

# CHAPTER NINE
## *The Road to Riches*

I hope this book has sparked your interest, and motivated you enough to go out and start up your own sales for profit business. By familiarizing yourself with the tips and rules to be followed to make your business a successful one, you should have no trouble getting your own business off the ground, and making that business everything you hope it will be.

The sales for profit business can be very rewarding when handled properly. The money to be made, and the freedom that money can provide, should be more than enough incentive to get you going. I know of what I speak. I've seen it firsthand, and the people I've met all enjoy what they do immensely.

As I've stated before, there are risks involved in the starting of any new business, but it is only the people willing to take those risks that will prosper. Whether you work in this business part-time or full-time, if you are selling merchandise people want to buy, you should find that your profits in this business far outweigh your expenses. By keeping up your confidence, even when sales are slow, and never giving up, you can create a life for yourself that others only dream of.

As you run your business, you will undoubtedly learn things not covered in this book, and even come up with a few techniques and rules of your own that will make running your new business easier and more profitable for you. When questions arise, don't hesitate to refer back to the chapters in this book that can help you, and take the advice to heart.

Everything you've read in this book is designed to get your new sales for profit business off to a running start, and keep it running at as smooth a pace as possible, so that you can reap maximum rewards. The information in this book is here to help you. Let it. Make your first steps on the road to riches just a little easier.

Since you decided to buy this book, I can only assume that you are one of the serious few determined to make a better life for yourself, and that you truly wish to create a prosperous business of your own. Keep your dreams in mind, never get discouraged, and keep looking ahead to keep those dreams of success on track.

If you have enjoyed this book, and it has helped you in any way, please leave a review. I would love to hear from you. I wish you all of the luck in the world with your new sales for profit business. Here's to wishing you happiness, health, and enough profits from your present and future sales to make all of your dreams come true!

*"Businesses are grown from ideas of all sizes. No idea is too big or too small."*

- *Joseph Pesta*

# ABOUT THE AUTHOR

Joseph Pesta is a business growth expert, author, and consultant. He is the owner of his own business and technology consulting firm, which has been providing companies with business, technology, and marketing solutions for over twenty years.

Through his work, Mr. Pesta has helped many businesses, individuals, and organizations reach their goals, and continues to work to provide business owners with the knowledge, skills, and tools they need to help keep their businesses vital, competitive, and growing in a landscape that keeps moving forward.

From online, to print, to video, he also works across several media outlets to provide resources and educational materials that are designed not only to assist those who wish to start their own businesses and realize their dreams, but to assist those who are struggling to overcome obstacles in their businesses, and help them get their businesses successfully back on track.

To learn more about Joseph Pesta, and his consulting firm, visit: www.josephpesta.com

Twitter: www.twitter.com/jpesta
Facebook: www.facebook.com/jpestaconsulting

# FREE NEWSLETTER

Be sure to get your FREE newsletter with the latest tips and tricks, new product and service announcements, exclusive discounts, free downloads, and more. Signing up is easy! Just enter your e-mail address, and that's it. See? We told you it would be easy. Don't miss out! Visit:

www.josephpesta.com

Start getting your FREE newsletter now!

## YOU MIGHT ALSO BE INTERESTED IN

## Sales for Profit - Companion Workbook & Journal

With the "Sales for Profit - Companion Workbook & Journal", you'll be given a useful tool with guidance from the author, along with forms, sections for your own notes, checklists, and more, all designed to keep your business organized and easy to manage. Be sure to grab your copy of the "Sales for Profit - Companion Workbook & Journal" today!

# TAKE YOUR BUSINESS
# TO THE NEXT LEVEL

Kick your business into high gear!  We offer a wide variety of services, all designed for you to get the most out of your business and reach the goals you wish to achieve.  Simply visit:

www.josephpesta.com

We're here to help, and we want to see you succeed!

# NOTES

# NOTES

# NOTES